Leo and the Paperbark

Leanne Murner

Illustrated by Kat Fox

Serenity Press Pty Ltd
Waikiki, WA 6169

First published by Serenity Press (Serenity Press Kids) in 2021
www.serenitypress.org

National Library of Australia
Cataloguing-in-Publication entry

Murner, Leanne (Leanne, Murner), Leo and the Paperbark Tree

ISBN: 978-0-6452689-2-8 (hc)

Leo and the Paperbark

Leanne Murner

Illustrated by Kat Fox

"Hey Poppy, what are you doing?" said Leo.

"I am just trimming a branch that has fallen," said Poppy John.

"Oh!" said Leo, "What is that peeling off the branch, Poppy?"

"That is the tree's bark, Leo. This tree is called a paperbark tree" said Poppy John.

"So the bark is paper? Can I draw on it?" said Leo.

"Yes Leo, you can draw or paint on it," said Poppy.

"This tree's bark has so many uses, Leo. It has been a great resource for people for thousands and thousands of years," said Poppy, "it can been used for painting or sending messages."

"It can be shaped into a bowl to carry water or to eat meals from."

"It can even be used wet to line the ground ovens to help with cooking food in the fire."

5

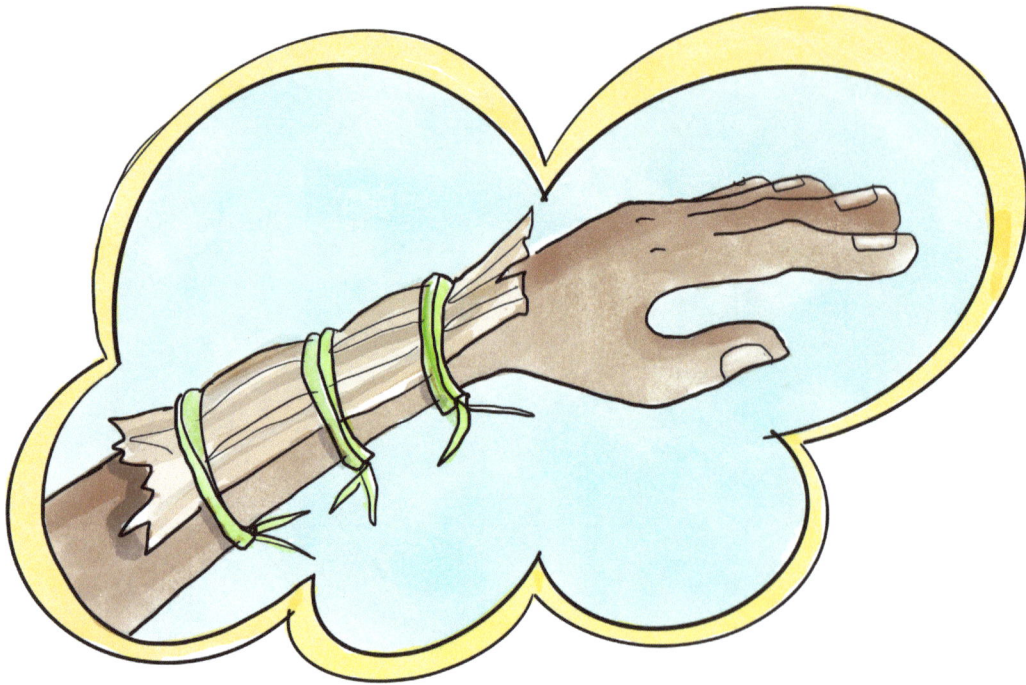

"It can be used as bandages for wounds when we're hurt."

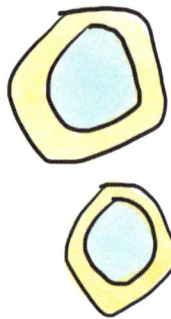

6

"It can be used as a temporary raincoat for protection from the weather."

"It can be used for roofing and shelters in the bush and even bedding for babies," Poppy said.

7

"See the layers of peeling bark, Leo? Under the bark is the trunk, there are so many layers of bark, this helps protect the main trunk from fire. During a fire the outside bark will burn, leaving the white inside layers that protect the tree," said Poppy John.

"After a fire the tree will produce new shoots to create foliage all over the tree," said Poppy John.

"See these leaves, Leo," said Poppy John, "the oil from the leaves can be used as an antiseptic and can be brewed to make a tea to treat head colds and headaches. This tree is a great source for medicine!"

"Did you know, Leo, these trees can live for up to 100 years and are a great for helping find water? They only grow where there is water in the ground. This is good to know when you're in the bush," said Poppy John.

"Some of the trees store water in their trunks with a water hump on the branch," said Poppy John.

"Water hump, what is that?" said Leo.

"See here Leo, this is a water hump," said Poppy.

13

"Here Leo, hold this bowl to catch the water from the tree. Stand back, I need to make a small hole at the bottom of the water hump for the water to come out," said Poppy.

"Here is comes Leo, hold the bowl underneath to catch the water."

"Oh wow, Poppy!" said Leo.

"Look at all the water in there Leo, all that was stored in the tree," said Poppy.

"How does the water get into the tree?" said Leo.

"All trees have roots in the ground and the roots will suck the water from the ground and store it in the trunk."

"If there is a drought and this tree needs some water, it can use some of the water that it took from the ground to survive."

"These trees can survive dry times as well as when it rains a lot," said Poppy John.

"What is the bird doing?" said Leo.

"Looks like he is having a drink," said Poppy, "it must have seen us getting the water from the tree."

"Oh, where is the bird going, Poppy?" said Leo.

"It has gone into the tree to drink some nectar from the flowers," said Poppy, "see all these flowers up there Leo, these are sometimes called bottlebrushes. These flowers turn into seeds once they have finished flowering."

"Look here, Leo," said Poppy, "can you see all these little flowers and all the little buds forming?"

"Yes, I can," said Leo.

"Capsules are starting to form, and hold heaps of little seeds," said Poppy.

"So if the birds eat the flowers, who eats the seeds?" said Leo.

"The seeds are safe in their capsules waiting for a chance to grow into a new tree!"

"See hanging up there in the tree, that is a fruit bat. Bats will eat the nectar," said Poppy.

"Bats will sleep all day and be up all night, these animals are called nocturnal animals," said Poppy.

"Poppy, can I take some bottlebrush flowers and paper bark bowl to school for show and tell?" said Leo.

"Yes ,that is a great idea, Leo!" said Poppy.

Paperbark Tree

There are over 300 species of melaleucas, most of which grow in Australia. Trees can live for over 100 years. We know the larger species as paperbarks, while the smaller are usually called honey myrtles.

Many birds and other creatures rely on melaleucas, such as little friarbirds, native bees, rosellas, scarlet honeyeaters, nankeen night herons, orange-bellied parrots and even orchids.

Paperbark Flowering Pod

Melaleuca flowers are usually arranged in spikes or heads. Within the head, the flowers are often in groups of two or three, each flower or group having a papery bract at its base. Their flowers also come in an amazing range of colours, from white, cream and yellow through to orange, red, pink and even purple.

Scarlet Honeyeater

The scarlet honeyeater is easy to spot with their bright red and black colouring with a white belly. They prefer open forests and woodlands, especially near wetlands. Their numbers may be declining across their range due to loss of mature habitat trees.

Scarlet honeyeaters seek out flowering natives like grevilleas and banksias in the colder months and turpentine, melaleuca and pittosporum trees in the warmer months. If you have these plants in your garden this little honeyeater will hover about to collect the nectar, tiny wings beating rapidly and the curved beak dipping in and out of flowers.

Orange-bellied Parrot

The orange-bellied parrot is a small, migratory ground parrot measuring about 20cm. They're a bright array of colours. Sadly, they're one of Australia's most threatened species. With up to 50 adults in the wild, they're at great risk of extinction.

The orange-bellied parrot is one of only three migratory parrot species in the world. From Tasmania, they migrate to coastal Victoria and South Australia to spend autumn and winter. They usually stay within 3km of the coastline to forage on coastal saltmarsh vegetation and adjacent weedy pastures.

The decline of the orange-bellied parrot is likely influenced by habitat loss. Changes to fire management practices in the breeding range may also have had an effect.

Fruit Bat

The fruit bat's long wings allow them to stay warm during roosting. They wrap up in their wings to conserve body heat. They live in large colonies because they feel safer with numbers. Most of them live in warmer climates where they can take advantage of various fruits that will grow throughout the year.

When the fruit bat roosts during the day, they do so high in the trees. This gives them darkness and it also protects them from various predators. They may hide in crevices and other dark spaces as well.

They don't eat all of the fruit's contents. Instead, they use their teeth to crush into the fruit. Then they will consume the nectar. The young will stay with their mother, even when she is out looking for food. They will cling to her body with claws that allow them to effortlessly remain in place. Bats can not fly until they are 6 weeks old.

Dedication

I would like to dedicate this book to my best friend and husband. Thank you for supporting me through this amazing journey.

My Leo for being my inspiration, Poppy John for his wealth of knowledge and support.

And to my amazing friend Amy for pushing me out of my comfort zone two years ago, starting my new life purpose.

I would not be here today without you believing in me.

About the Author

Leanne Murner is an author, business owner/designer at 5 Little Bears Pty Ltd and a proud mum of five boys. Leanne saw a gap in the market for Australian themed wooden toys and began creating products for children with an educational and Australian twist. Being a creative soul Leanne grew the business fast and as time went by her product portfolio increased. In addition she has also published the first two of a series of six children's books, Franki and the Banskia, and Loui and the Grass Tree, with the remaining being published this year. Leanne wanted to teach kids about Australian native flora and fauna, what they are and who needs them to survive. Leanne is busy working on another series of books teaching kids about Australian animals and their habitat, threats and how we can help. Leanne is passionate that our children need to be better educated on Australian wildlife to help keep it from extinction.

www.ingramcontent.com/pod-product-compliance
Lightning Source LLC
Chambersburg PA
CBHW042009090426
42811CB00015B/1594